Table of

Fan's Dictionary
Song

About This Book 3
A 5
B 10
C 11
D 14
E 18
F 21
G 24
H 27
I 30
J 38
K 40
L 41
M 45
N 50
O 52
P 54
Q 56
R 57
S 60

T 70
V 80
W 81
Y 99

Over the years Watford F.C. fans have created incredible atmospheres in football grounds and come up with some of the creative chants and songs. This book is a guide for these chants and songs written by the Watford F.C. supporters.

From the Famous WFC, Football Club in History, Hoist Up The Watford Flag, Since I Was Young, We're The Horns, You Are My Watford to songs dedicated to the various players and staff, the very best of the terrace chants, songs, and timeless classics, this book will delight and entertain in equal measure and honors every single Watford F.C. fan who has ever sung in support for the team throughout its proud history.

All the songs and chants in this book are written and sang by the Watford F.C. supporters during football matches, at pubs and bars or posted to message boards, they are not the thoughts or views of the authors.

WRITE TO US

We greatly value your opinion. We would love to hear your thoughts and recommendations about this book so we can improve! Write to us: fansdictionary@gmail.com

COPYRIGHT

Copyright © 2022 by Fan's Dictionary

The author has provided this book only for personal use. Thank you for buying and for complying with copyright laws by not reproducing, scanning, or distributing any part of it in any form without permission.

ABDOULAYE DOUCOURÉ

(To the of tune of September by Earth, Wind & Fire)

1,2,3,4,
Ooooo Abdoulaye Doucouré,
Ooooo Abdoulaye Doucouré,
Ooooo Abdoulaye Doucouré...

ADAM MASINA

(To the tune of La Bamba by Los Lobos)

Adam Masina,
Adam Masina,
He eats spaghetti,
He drinks Moretti,
His c*ck's f**king massive...

ADRIAN MARIAPPA

(To the of tune of Do The Conga)

Do do do we've got Mariappa,
Do do do he's gonna score a goal,
Do do do we've got Mariappa,
Do do do he's gonna score a goal...

AIDY BOOTHROYD

(To the tune of Hey Jude by The Beatles)

Hey Boothroyd don't be afraid,
Take a sh*t team and make it better,
Remember to sign Marlon King,
Then we will win,
And make it better, better, better, better...
Na na na nananananana Watford.

AL BANGURA

Bang Bang Bang,
Al Bangura,
Bang Bang Bang,
Al Bangura...

ALL WE WANT IS ONE SONG

(To the tune of Bread of Heaven)

All we want,
All we want,
All we want is just one song...

ALMEN ABDI

(To the tune of No Limit by 2 Unlimited)

Abdi, Almen Abdi, Almen Abdi, Almen Abdi, Abdi...

(To the tune of I'm Gonna Be 500 Miles)

And I would walk 500 miles,
And I would walk 500 more,
Just to see that man from Switzerland,
Run and pass and shoot and score.

Almen Abdi, Almen Abdi,
Almen Abdi, Almen Abdi,
Der-der-der, der-der-der, der-der-der.

AND IT'S WATFORD FC

(To the tune of The Wild Rover)

And it's Watford FC,
Watford FC,
We're by far the greatest team,
The world has ever seen...

ARE YOU WATCHING

(To the tune of Bread of Heaven)

Are you watching,
Are you watching,
Are you watching Luton Town,
Are you watching Luton Town...

AWAY IN A MANGER

(To the tune of Away in a Manger)

Away in a manger,
No crib for his bed,
The little Lord Jesus looked up and he said,
F**k of Luton Town,
F**k of Luton Town...

BERTIE MEE SAID

(To the tune of Bertie Mee Said To Bill Shankly)

Bertie Mee said to Ken Furphy,
Have you heard of the North Bank Highbury,
Ken said no, I don't think so,
But I've heard of the Watford Rookery...

BUILD A BONFIRE

(To the tune of Oh my Darling Clementine)

Build a bonfire,
Build a bonfire,
Put the Luton on the top,
Put Bournemouth in the middle,
And we'll burn the f**king lot.

CAN WE PLAY YOU EVERY WEEK

(To the tune of Bread of Heaven)

Can we play you,
Can we play you,
Can we play you every week,
Can we play you every week...

CHAMPIONS LEAGUE

(To the tune of Tom Hark by Piranhas)

Champions League you're having a laugh,
Champions League you're having a laugh,
Champions League you're having a laugh...

CLINT EASTON

Woooewooewooo, Clint Easton...

COME IN A TAXI

(To the tune of Guantanamera)

Come in a taxi,
You must of come in a taxi,
Come in a taxi,
You must of come in a taxi...

COULDN'T SELL YOUR TICKETS

(To the tune of Guantanamera)

Sell all your tickets,
You couldn't sell all your tickets,
Sell all your tickets,
You couldn't sell all your tickets...

CRISTIAN BATTOCCHIO

(To the tune of Sloop John B by Beach Boys)

He's not from Japan,
He's not from Japan,
Christian Ba-Tokyo,
He's not from Japan...

CRY IN A MINUTE

(To the tune of Guantanamera)

Cry in a minute,
You're gonna cry in a minute,
Cry in a minute,
You're gonna cry in a minute...

DANNY GRAHAM

(To the tune of He's Got The Whole World In His Hands)

Top scorer in the league,
We've got the top scorer in the league,
We've got the top scorer in the league,
We've got the top scorer in the league...

DANNY ROSE

(To the of tune of Daddy Cool)

Danny, Danny Rose,
Danny, Danny Rose,
Danny, Danny Rose,
Danny, Danny Rose...

DANNY SHITTU

(To the tune of Chim Chim Cher-ee)

Chim chiminney, chim chim cheroo,
Who needs Sol Campbell,
When we've got Shittu...

DARIUS HENDERSON

Henderson, Henderson,
Henderson, Henderson...

DAVID PLEATS

(To the tune of My Old Man's a Dustman)

David Pleats a w**ker,
He wears a w**kers hat,
And when he wears the w**kers hat,
He looks like a flippin p***.

DIRTY NORTHERNERS

Go down pub,
Drink 10 pints and get absolutely plastered,
Go back home and beat the wife,
You dirty northern b**tards.

You dirty northern b**tards,
You dirty northern b**tards,
You dirty northern b**tards...

DO YOU REMEMBER 3 NIL

(To Leeds, to the tune of Blue Moon)

3 nil,
Do you remember 3 nil,
Do you remember 3 nil,
Do you remember 3 nil...

DO YOU SPEAK ENGLISH

(To the tune of La Donna È Mobile)

Do you speak English,
Do you speak English,
Do you speak English,
Do you speak English...

DYNAMITE

Luther's black and Ross is white,
They are f**king dynamite...

EIEIEIO

(To the tune of Knees up Mother Brown)

EIEIEIO, up the football league we go,
When we get promotion,
This is what we'll sing,
We've got Marlon, we've got Marlon,
We've got Marlon King...

ELTON JOHN

Elton John is having a party,
Bring your vodka and some charlie...

(And)

Elton John's Taylor Made Army,
Elton John's Taylor Made Army,
Elton John's Taylor Made Army,
Elton John's Taylor Made Army...

(To the tune of The Quartermaster's Stores)

He's queer, he's bent,
His a*se is up for rent,
Elton John, Elton John...

He's bald, he's bent,
He pays the f**king rent,
Elton John, Elton John...

ETIENNE CAPOUE

(To the tune of Achy Breaky Heart)

We've got Capoue,
Etienne Capoue,
I just don't think you understand,
He's Walters man,
He's better than Zidane,
We've got Etienne Capoue...

EVERYWHERE WE GO

Everywhere we go,
Everywhere we go,
People want to know,
People want to know,
Who we are,
Who we are,
Where we come from,
Where we come from,
Shall we tell them,
Shall we tell them,
Who we are,
Who we are,
Where we come from,
Where we come from,
We are the Watford,
We are the Watford,
We are the army,
We are the army,
Malky's army...

FAMOUS WFC

(To the tune of Lord of the Dance)

Watford wherever we may be,
We are the boys from the Rookery,
And we don't give a f**k,
Who ever you may be,
'Cos we are the famous WFC...

FERNANDO FORESTIERI

(To the tune of The White Stripes by Seven Nation Army)

Ohhh Forestieri,
Ohhh Forestieri,
Ohhh Forestieri,
Ohhh Forestieri...

FITZ HALL

One size Fitz Hall,
One size Fitz Hall,
One size Fitz Hall,
One size Fitz Hall...

FOOTBALL CLUB IN HISTORY

(To the tune of Z Cars Theme)

1 2 3 we've got the best team,
WFC the club for me,
Can't you see that we're the greatest,
Football club in histor-history.

Someone said that you're a good team,
WFC wont let it be,
You will see that we're the greatest,
Football club in histor-history...

...Come on lads let's have some action,
We can show them what to do,
If you sing it, we're the greatest,
Football club in histor-history.

WFC we've got them going,
Home with nothing for their tea,
Come on sing it, we're the greatest,
Football club in histor-history.

GARY PORTER

Gary, Gary Porter,
Gary, Gary Porter...

GAVIN MAHON

(To the tune of Volare)

When your sitting in row Z,
And the ball hits your head,
Gavin Mahon, Gavin Mahon...

(To the tune of The Quartermaster's Stores)

He shot, he missed,
He must be f**king pissed,
Gavin Mahon, Gavin Mahon.

GET TO WORK

(To the tune of Bread of Heaven)

Get to work,
Get to work,
Get to work you lazy t*ats,
Get to work you lazy t*ats...

GIANFRANCO ZOLA

(To the tune of Volare)

Gianfranco Woah,
Gianfranco Woah,
He's only 5 foot 3,
He comes from Italy...

(To the tune of Take Me Home, Country Road)

Gianfranco take me home,
To the place, I belong,
Hertfordshire, Vicarage Road,
Take me home, Gianfranco...

(To the tune of Lola by The Kinks)

He only grew to 5 foot 3,
That's 'cos he comes from Italy,
I say Zola, oh oh oh oh Zola...

GRAHAM TAYLOR

Ooh ahh Graham Taylor,
Ooh ahh Graham Taylor,
Ooh ahh Graham Taylor...

HEIDAR HELGUSON

(To the tune of Hooray! Hooray!
It's a Holi-Holiday)

Heidar Helguson,
Heidar Helguson,
Heidar, Heidar, Heidar Helguson,
He gets the ball, he scores a goal,
Heidar, Heidar, Heidar Helguson...

HAVE YOU FOUND YOUR REVISION

(To the tune of The White Stripes by
Seven Nation Army)

Have you found your revision,
Have you found your revision,
Have you found your revision...

HELLO HELLO

(To the tune of Marching Through Georgia)

Hello, Hello, we are the Watford boys,
Hello, Hello, we are the Watford boys,
If you are a Luton fan,
Surrender or you die,
We all follow the Watford...

HOIST UP THE WATFORD FLAG

(To the tune of Sloop John B by Beach Boys)

Hoist up the Watford flags,
Hear all the Hornets sing,
And if you don't join in I'll sing on my own,
I don't wanna go home, I don't wanna go home,
This is the best trip, I've ever been on...

I CAN'T READ AND I CAN'T WRITE

I can't read and I can't write,
But that dosen't really matter,
'Cos I come up from Hertfordshire,
And I can drive a tractor...

I HEAR THE SOUND

(To the tune of Distant Bums by Jim Reeves)

I hear the sound,
Of Distant Bums,
Over there,
Over there,
And do they smell,
Like f**king hell.

I LOVE TO GO A-WANDERING

(To the tune of The Happy Wanderer)

I love to go a-wandering,
To see what I can wreck,
And if I see a Luton fan,
I'll break his f**king neck.

I WANNA GO HOME

(To the tune of Sloop John B by Beach Boys)

I wanna go home,
I wanna go home,
Leeds is a sh*t hole,
I wanna go home...

I WAS BORN UNDER

(To the tune of I Was Born Under a Wandering Star)

I was born under a Rookery roof,
I was born under a Rookery roof,
Where coppers were made to fight,
And guns were made to shoot,
If you come down the Rookery,
We'll all stick in the boot...

IF YOU ALL LOVE WATFORD

(To the tune of If You're Happy and You Know It)

If you all love Watford clap your hands,
If you all love Watford clap your hands,
All love Watford, all love Watford,
All love Watford clap your hands...

IF YOU GO DOWN TO THE WOODS

(To the tune of The Teddy Bear's Picnic)

If you go down to the woods today,
You better go in disguise,
If you go down to the woods today,
You're sure of a big surprise,
'Cos Jeremy the sugar puffs bear,
Has got some boots and cropped his hair,
Today's the day that Jeremy joins the Rookery.

IKECHI ANYA

(To the tune of Heartbeat)

Ikechi,
Ikechi Anya,
Runs down the wing for me,
Duh duh, duh duh duh…

I'M AN ORNET

I'm an Ornet, I'm an Ornet,
I'm an Ornet through and through,
I'm an Ornet, I'm an Ornet,
And I don't give a f**k about you.

IMRAN LOUZA

(To the of tune of Don't You Want Me
by The Human League)

Imran Louza baby,
Imran Louza woah,
Imran Louza baby,
Imran Louza woah…

IS THERE A FIRE DRILL

(To the tune of La Donna È Mobile)

Is there a fire drill,
Is there a fire drill,
Is there a fire drill,
Is there a fire drill...

IS THIS A LIBRARY

(To the tune of La Donna È Mobile)

Is this a library,
Is this a library,
Is this a library,
Is this a library...

ISMAILA SARR

(To the tune of Logical Song by Supertramp)

Oh Ismaila Sarr oh he is so wonderful,
When he scores a goal,
Oh it's beautiful, magical,
When he runs down the wing
He's as fast as lightning, he's frightening,
And he makes all the Horns sing...

IT'S ALL QUIET

(To the tune of If You're Happy And You Know It)

It's all gone quiet over there,
All gone quiet over there,
All gone quiet, all gone quiet,
It's all gone quiet over there...

IT'S ALL YOUR FAULT

It's all your fault, It's all your fault,
It's all your fault, It's all your fault...

IT'S SPRING AGAIN

It's spring again, we'll sing again,
B**locks to Luton Town,
With a heart so true, I'll sing to you,
B**locks to Luton Town...

IS IT TRUE

Luton Town,
Luton Town,
Is it true what people say you're going
down,
Oh Luton Town...

JOBI MCANUFF

(To the tune of Give It Up by KC & The Sunshine Band)

Nananana Jobi McAnuff,
McAnuff, Jobi McAnuff,
Nananana Jobi McAnuff,
McAnuff, Jobi McAnuff,
Nananana Jobi McAnuff,
McAnuff, Jobi McAnuff....

JOHN EUSTACE

Johnny Eustace,
Johnny, Johnny, Eustace,
Johnny Eustace,
Johnny, Johnny, John...

(To the tune of Can't Take My Eyes Off You)

Oh Johnny Eustace,
You are the love of my life,
Oh Johnny Eustace,
I'd let you s*ag my wife,
Oh Johnny Eustace,
I want curly hair too..

JONATHAN HOGG

(To the tune of Tom Hark)

Jonathan Hogg,
Jonathan Hogg
Jonathan Hogg
Jonathan Hogg...

KEN SEMA

(To the tune of Oh Sit Down by James)

Ken Sema,
Ken Sema,
Running down the wing,
Sema-ma-ma-ma-ma-ma,
The Swedish King...

LA LA LA WATFORD

(To the tune of Carnival de Paris)

La la la la la la la la la la Watford...

LALALALALALA WATFORD

(To the tune of Hey Jude)

La la la lalalalalala lalala, lalala Watford...

LET'S ALL HAVE A DISCO

(To the tune of The Conga)

Let's all have a disco,
Let's all have a disco,
Na na na na,
Na na na na....

LET'S GO MENTAL

(To the tune of The Conga)

Let's go f**king mental,
Let's go f**king mental,
Na na na na,
Na na na na....

LINESMAN

(To the tune of Bread of Heaven)

Whose the w*nker with the flag,
Whose the w*nker with the flag,
Whose the w*nker,
Whose the w*nker,
Whose the w*nker with the flag...

LIVERPOOL SLUMS

(To the tune of In My Liverpool Home)

In your Liverpool slums,
You look in the dustbins for something to eat,
You find a dead rat and you think it's a treat,
In your Liverpool slums...

LLOYD DOYLEY

(To the tune of La Donna È Mobile)

We've got Lloydinho,
We've got Lloydinho,
We've got Lloydinho,
We've got Lloydinho...

LUTON BOYS

Luton boys,
Make more noise,
Playing with their Tonka toys,
Lalalalalala...

LUTON SING

The Luton sing,
I don't know why,
'Cos after the game,
They're going to die...

MALKY MACKAY

(To the tune of Tom Hark by Piranhas)

Malky Mackay,
Malky Mackay,
He's having a beer,
And he's having a pie...

MALKY'S TAYLOR MADE ARMY

Malky's Taylor Made Army,
Malky's Taylor Made Army,
Malky's Taylor Made Army,
Malky's Taylor Made Army...

MALKY'S YELLOW ARMY

Malky's Yellow Army,
Malky's Yellow Army,
Malky's Yellow Army...

MANUEL ALMUNIA

(To the tune of La Donna È Mobile)

Manuel Almunia,
Manuel Almunia,
Manuel Almunia,
Manuel Almunia...

MARCO CASSETTI

(To the tune of Oh Sit Down by James)

Marco Cassetti,
Marco Cassetti,
Running down the wing,
Hear the Hornets Sing,
Marco Cassetti...

MICAH HYDE

(To the tune of The Quartermaster's Stores)

He's here,
He's there,
He's every f**king where,
Micah Hyde, Micah Hyde...

MICHEL NGONGE

(To the tune of Kumbaya My Lord)

Ngonge my Lord, Ngonge,
Ngonge my Lord, Ngonge,
Ngonge my Lord, Ngonge,
Oh Lord Ngonge.

MOUSSA SISSOKO

(To the tune of The White Stripes by Seven Nation Army)

Oh Moussa Sissoko,
Oh Moussa Sissoko,
Oh Moussa Sissoko...

MY GARDEN SHED

(To the tune of When the Saints Go Marching In)

My garden shed,
(My garden shed),
Is bigger than this,
(Is bigger than this),
My garden shed is bigger than this,
It's got a door, and a window,
My garden shed is bigger this...

MY OLD MAN

(To the tune of My Old Man)

My old man said be a Luton fan,
And I said b**locks you're a c*nt,
I'd rather sh*g a bucket with a big hole in it,
Than be a Luton fan for just one minute,
With hammers and hatchets, stanley knives and spanners,
We'll show the City b**tards how to fight,
(How to fight),
I'd rather sh*g a bucket with a big hole in it,
Than be a Luton fan,
Altogether now...

NEIL COX

Neil down if you love our Cox...

NEIL WARNOCK

Warnock is a w*nker,
Warnock is a w*nker,
Nanana, nanana...

NICK WRIGHT

Oh Nicky Wright,
Back in May in 1999,
Smarty scored a goal in added time,
I remember Nicky Wright...

NIGEL PEARSON

(To the tune of Bad Moon Rising)

We've got Super Nigel Pearson,
He knows exactly what we need,
Catcart at the back,
Deeney in the attack,
Pearson's keeping us,
In the Premier League.

NYRON NOSWORTHY

(To the tune of Rehab by Amy Winehouse)

You try to get the ball past Nyron,
But he said,
No, no, no...

ODION IGHALO

(To the tune of Gold by Spandau Ballet)

Ighalo, always believe in your soul,
You've got the power to know,
You're indestructible,
Always believe in, Ighalo...

OH WHEN THE ORNS

(To the tune of When The Saints Go Marching In)

Oh when the Orns,
(Oh when the Orns),
Go steaming in,
(Go steaming in),
Oh when the Orns go steaming in,
I wanna be in that number,
Oh when the Orns go steaming in...

OLE'S AT THE WHEEL

(To Manchester United)

Ole's at the wheel, at the wheel,
Ole's at the wheel, lalalalala...

ONE NIL

(To the tune of Go West)

1-0 to the Golden Boys,
1-0 to the Golden Boys,
1-0 to the Golden Boys,
1-0 to the Golden Boys...

1-0 and you still don't sing,
1-0 and you still don't sing,
1-0 and you still don't sing,
1-0 and you still don't sing...

POOR LITTLE HATTER

(To the tune of I'm Only a Poor Little Sparrow)

He's only a poor little hatter,
His face is all tattered and torn,
He made me feel sick,
So I hit him with a brick,
And now he don't sing anymore...

POSH SPICE

(To the tune of My Old Man's A Dustman)

Oh Posh Spice is sla**er,
She loves it in the box,
And when she's s*agging David,
She dreams of Neil Cox...

QUE SERA SERA

(To the tune of Que Sera Sera)

Que sera, sera,
Whatever will be, will be,
We're going to Wembley,
Que sera, sera...

QUIQUE SANCHEZ FLORES

Oooo Quique Sanchez Flores,
Oooo oooo Quique Sanchez Flores,
Oooo Quique Sanchez Flores,
Oooo oooo Quique Sanchez Flores...

RICHARLISON

(To the tune of La Bamba)

Richarlison, Richarlison,
Oh Richarlison, oh Richarlison,
Plays for Watford in Silva's Army...

ROCKET MAN

(To the tune of Rocket Man by Elton John)

She packed my bags last night pre-flight,
Zero hour 9:00 a.m and I'm gonna be high,
As a kite by then,
I miss the Earth so much I miss my wife,
It's lonely out in space,
On such a timeless flight,
And I think it's gonna be a long, long time,
Til touchdown brings me around again to find...

...I'm not the man they think I am at home,
Oh, no, no, no, I'm a rocket man,
Rocket man, burning out his fuse up here alone,
And I think it's gonna be a long, long time,
Til touchdown brings me 'round again to find,
I'm not the man they think I am at home,
Oh, no, no, no, I'm a rocket man,
Rocket man, burning out his fuse up here alone,
Mars ain't the kind of place to raise your kids,
In fact it's cold as hell,
And there's no one there to raise them,
If you did and all this science,
I don't understand,
It's just my job five days a week,
A rocket man, a rocket man,
And I think it's gonna be a long, long time...

...Til touchdown brings me around again to find,
I'm not the man they think I am at home
Oh, no, no, no, I'm a rocket man,
Rocket man, burning out his fuse up here alone,
And I think it's gonna be a long, long time,
Til touchdown brings me 'round again to find,
I'm not the man they think I am at home,
Oh, no, no, no, I'm a rocket man,
Rocket man, burning out his fuse up here alone,
And I think it's gonna be a long, long time,
And I think it's gonna be a long, long time,
And I think it's gonna be a long, long time,
And I think it's gonna be a long, long time,
And I think it's gonna be a long, long time,
And I think it's gonna be a long, long time,
And I think it's gonna be a long, long time,
And I think it's gonna be a...

SH*T GROUND NO FANS

(To the tune of Big Ben Chimes)

Sh*t ground no fans,
Sh*t ground no fans,
Sh*t ground no fans,
Sh*t ground no fans...

SACKED IN THE MORNING

(To the tune of Guantanamera)

Sacked in the morning,
You're getting sacked in the morning,
Sacked in the morning,
You're getting sacked in the morning...

SAME OLD

(To the tune of Big Ben Chimes)

Same old Arsenal, always cheating,
Same old Arsenal, always cheating...

SCARS OUT

(To the tune of The Conga)

Let's all get our scars out,
Let's all get our scars out,
La la la la,
La la la la...

SCOTT FITZGERALD

He came from Northwood Town,
He only cost a pound,
Fitzgerald, woahhh....

SHE WORE A YELLOW RIBBON

(To the tune of She Wore a Yellow Ribbon)

She wore, she wore, she wore a yellow ribbon,
She wore a yellow ribbon in the merry month of May,
And when I asked why she wore that ribbon,
She said it's for Watford and we're going to Wembley,
Wembley, Wembley,
We're the famous Watford FC,
And we're going to Wembley,
Wembley, Wembley...

SIGH NO MORE

(To the tune of Sigh No More Ladies Sigh No More)

Sigh no more, Hornets, sigh no more,
Horns were deceivers ever,
One foot in sea and one on shore,
To one thing constant never,
Then sigh not so,
But let them go,
And be you blithe and bonny,
Converting all your sounds of woe,
Into...
Hey Nonny, Nonny, hey Nonny, Nonny...

SINCE I WAS YOUNG

Since I was Young,
I followed them,
Watford FC, the team for me...

SING WHEN YOU'RE WINNING

(To the tune of Guantanamera)

Sing when you're winning,
You only sing when you're winning,
Sing when you're winning,
You only sing when you're winning...

SING YOUR HEARTS OUT

(To the tune of Bread of Heaven)

Sing your hearts out,
Sing your hearts out,
Sing your hearts out for the lads,
Sing your hearts out for the lads...

SIT DOWN AND READ

(To the tune of Go West)

Sit down and read your books,
Sit down and read your books,
Sit down and read your books
Sit down and read your books...

SIT DOWN LEEDS SCUM

Sit down Leeds scum,
Sit down Leeds scum,
Sit down Leeds scum...

SIT DOWN SHUT UP

Sit down shut up,
Sit down shut up,
Sit down shut up...

SMALL TOWN IN SCUNTHORPE

(To the tune of Guantanamera)

Small town in Scunthorpe,
You're just a small town in Scunthorpe,
Small town in Scunthorpe,
You're just a small town in Scunthorpe...

SPELL IT OUT

(Single bloke) Give us a W (Crowd) W,
(Single bloke) A (Crowd) A,
(Single bloke) T (Crowd) T,
(Single bloke) F (Crowd) F,
(Single bloke) O (Crowd) O,
(Single bloke) R (Crowd) R,
(Single bloke) D (Crowd) D,
And what have you got,
The Watford,
The Watford...

STAND UP

(To the tune of Go West)

Stand up if you're looking good,
Stand up if you're looking good,
Stand up if you're looking good...

Stand up if you love Watford,
Stand up if you love Watford,
Stand up if you love Watford...

Stand up if you've paid your tax,
Stand up if you've paid your tax,
Stand up if you've paid your tax...

Stand up if you can't sit down,
Stand up if you can't sit down,
Stand up if you can't sit down...

STEVE PALMER

(To the tune of Winter Wonderland)

There's only one Steve Palmer,
And he smokes Marijuana,
Walking along,
Hooting a bong,
Walkin in a Palmer wonderland...

STEWARDS

We don't care about stewards,
They don't care about me,
All I care about is Watford FC...

STICK YOUR CAMERA

(To the tune of If You're Happy and You Know It)

You can stick your f**king camera up your a*se,
You can stick your f**king camera up your a*se,
You can stick your f**king camera,
Stick your f**king camera,
Stick your f**king camera up your a*se.

SUPER SUPER

(To the tune of Skip To My Lou)

Super Super Dan,
Super Super Dan,
Super Super Dan,
Super Danny Graham...

TAKE MY ADVICE

(To the tune of Messing About on the River)

We've been up to Wolves to fight the North Bank,
We went up to Luton they weren't worth a w*nk,
So take my advice, there's nothing as nice,
As kicking the f**k out of Luton.

TAMAS PRISKIN

(To the tune of Na Na Hey Hey by Bananarama)

Lalalala,
Lalalala,
Whey hey Tamas Priskin...

TEN OF YOU SINGING

(To the tune of Guantanamera)

Ten of you singing,
There's only ten of you singing,
Ten of you singing,
There's only ten of you singing...

THAT BOY FERNANDO

(To the tune of Sloop John B by
Beach Boys, to Fernando Forestieri)

He's one of our own,
He's one of our own,
That boy Fernando,
He's one of our own...

THAT'S WHY

(To the tune of La Donna È Mobile)

That's why we're top of the league,
That's why we're top of the league,
That's why we're top of the league...

THE BEST BEHAVED SUPPORTERS

(To the tune of She'll Be Coming Round The Mountain)

We're the best behaved supporters in the land,
We're the best behaved supporters in the land,
We're the best behaved supporters,
Best behaved supporters,
Best behaved supporters in the land
(When we win)...

THE LUTON FANS

(To the tune of The Ants Go Marching)

The Luton fans came over the hill,
(Hurrah Hurrah),
The Luton fans came over the hill,
(Hurrah Hurrah),
The Luton fans came over the hill,
Saw the Watford standing still,
So they ran, ran, ran back to Luton town...

THE WATFORD WILL RISE

Pride of the north,
C*ck of the of the south,
We hate the Luton,
'Cos they are all mouth,
We took the Oak Road, that was f**k all,
The Watford will rise,
And the Luton will fall.

THERE'S A TEAM CALLING ME

(To the tune of The Littlest Hobo)

There's a team, that keeps calling me,
Down by the Vic.
That's where I'll Always be,
Every Goal we score,
We'll give out a roar,
Can't stand it now,
I'm going mad,
My golden Friends...

THIRTY QUID

(To the tune of Tom Hark by Piranhas)

Thirty quid, you're having a laugh,
Thirty quid, you're having a laugh,
Thirty quid, you're having a laugh...

THOSE WERE THE DAYS

(To the tune of Those Were The Days)

Once upon a time in the Red Lion,
We would raise a glass or two,
Remember how we laughed away the hours,
Talking about the scum we used to do...

Those were the days my friend,
We took the Oak Road End,
And run the scum, all over Harpenden,
Day or night, we stayed to fight,
Those were the days,
Those were the f**king days,
Na na na na na na na...

THREE NIL

(To the tune of Go West)

3-0 even Chambers scored,
3-0 even Chambers scored,
3-0 even Chambers scored,
3-0 even Chambers scored...

3-0 on your big day out,
3-0 on your big day out,
3-0 on your big day out,
3-0 on your big day out...

TOMMIE HOBAN

(To the tune of Sloop John B by Beach Boys)

He isn't on loan, he isn't on loan,
That Tommie Hoban, he isn't on loan...

TOMMY SMITH

(To the tune of Hooray! Hooray! It's a Holi-Holiday)

Tommy Smith, Tommy Smith,
Tommy Tommy Smith,
He gets the ball,
He scores a goal,
Tommy Tommy Smith...

TROY DEENEY

(To the tune of The Animals Went In Two By Two)

Lalalalalalalalalalalalalala la la,
Lalalalalalallalaalallalallala la la,
Lalalalalalalalala,
Troy Deeney,
Watford's number 9...

(To the tune of Sloop John B by Beach Boys)

He hates the police,
He hates the police,
That boy Troy Deeney,
He hates the police.

(To the of tune of Spirit in the Sky)

Deeney's a Legend forever more,
He drives a Lambo, he always scores,
Leicester tried to take him away,
But he said f**k off I wanna stay...

(and)

Deeney, Deeney, Deeney, Deeney...

VALON BEHRAMI

(To the tune of La Bamba)

Valon Behrami,
Valon Behrami,
(Oh, Valon Behrami),
Oh Valon Behrami,
Plays for Watford in Walter's army...

WATFORD

(To the tune of Boom Boom Boom by The Outhere Brothers)

Boom boom boom let me hear you say,
Watford, Watford,
De dum dum let me hear you say,
Watford, Watford...

WATFORD CLAP CLAP

Watford clap clap,
Watford clap clap,
With in goal Almunia and up front Bomber Otter...

WATFORD FC

Watford FC, Watford FC,
Watford FC, Watford FC, Watford FC...

WATFORD IS THE GREATEST

As I was walking down,
The Vatican one day,
I saw the Pope upon the steps,
And he began to pray,
I asked him what he's doing here,
And then I asked him why,
He lifted up his crucifix and gave me this reply...

We're on the march with Aidy's Army,
We're all going to Wemberlee,
And we'll realy shake them up,
When we win the FA cup,
'Cos Watford are the greatest football team.

WATFORD TILL I DIE

(To the tune of H-A-P-P-Y)

Watford till I die,
I'm Watford till I die,
I know I am,
I'm sure I am,
I'm Watford till I die...

WE ALL FOLLOW THE WATFORD

(To the tune of Land of Hope and Glory)

We all follow the Watford,
Over land and sea,
We all follow the Watford,
On to victory,
All together now...

WE ALL HATE LEEDS SCUM

(To the tune of Tom Hark by Piranhas)

We all hate Leeds scum,
We all hate Leeds scum,
We all hate Leeds scum,
We all hate Leeds scum...

WE ARE TOP OF THE LEAGUE

We are top of the league,
I said we are top of the league,
We are top of the league,
I said we are top of the league,
We are top of the league...

WE ARE 'ORNS

(To the of tune of We Are Young by Fun)

Tonight, we are 'Orns,
Oh Bassini you're a liar,
You weren't our real buyer,
You scum c*nt...

WE CAN SEE YOU SNEAKING OUT

(To the tune of Bread of Heaven)

We can see you,
We can see you,
We can see you sneaking out,
We can see you sneaking out...

WE FORGOT YOU

(To the tune of Bread of Heaven)

We forgot,
We forgot,
We forgot that you were here,
We forgot that you were here...

WE HAD JOY WE HAD FUN

(To the tune of Seasons In The Sun by Terry Jacks)

We had joy, we had fun,
We had Luton on the run,
But the joy didn't last,
'Cos the b**tards ran too fast...

WE LOVE YOU WATFORD

We love you Watford, we do,
We love you Watford, we do,
We love you Watford, we do,
Oh, Watford we love you...

WE LOVE YOU WE LOVE YOU

(To the tune of I Will Follow Him by Little Peggy March)

We love you, we love you, we love you,
And where you play,
We'll follow, we'll follow, we'll follow,
'Cos we support,
The Hornets, The Hornets, The Hornets,
And that's the way,
We like it, we like it, we like it,
Woaaah...

WE PAID FOR YOUR HATS

(To the tune of Sloop John B by Beach Boys)

We paid for your hats,
We paid for your hats,
What a waste of council tax,
We paid for your hats...

WE PAY YOUR BENEFITS

(To the tune of La Donna È Mobile)

We pay your benefits,
We pay your benefits,
We pay your benefits,
We pay your benefits...

WE PLAY ON THE FLOOR

(To the tune of Sloop John B by Beach Boys)

We play on the floor,
We play on the floor,
F**k off with your hoofball,
We play on the floor...

WE'LL MEET YOU AT THE STATION

Well we'll meet you at the station,
And you'd better bring a bottle,
'Cos there'll be some aggravation,
At the station...

WE'LL SIGN WHO WE WANT

(To the tune of Sloop John B by Beach Boys)

We'll sign who we want,
We'll sign who we want,
From Udinese,
We'll sign who we want...

WE'RE GONNA FIGHT

From the banks of bonny Scotland to the steps of the Rookery,
We're gonna fight, fight, fight,
For the Ornets till we win Division One,
To hell with Queens Park Rangers,
B**locks to Luton Town,
We're gonna fight, fight, fight,
For the Ornets till we win Division One.

WE'RE GONNA WIN 2-1

(To the tune of Blue Moon)

2-1,
We're gonna win 2-1,
We're gonna win 2-1,
We're gonna win 2-1...

WE'RE THE HORNS

(To the tune of Stars and Stripes Forever)

We're the Horns, we're the Horns, we're the Horns,
We're the Horns, we're the Horns, we're the Horns,
We're the Horns, we're the Horns, we're the Horns,
We're the Horns...

WE'RE THE REASON

(To the tune of Bread of Heaven)

We're the reason,
We're the reason,
We're the reason you are sh*te,
We're the reason you are sh*te...

WHAT DO WE THINK OF LUTON

(Bloke) What do we think of Luton,
(Crowd) Sh*t,
(Bloke) What do we think of sh*t,
(Crowd) Luton,
(Bloke) Thank you,
(Crowd) That's alright...

WHAT THE HELL WAS THAT

(To the tune of Bread of Heaven)

What the f**king,
What the f**king,
What the f**king hell was that,
What the f**king hell was that...

WHEN I WAS A LITTLE BOY

When I was a little boy,
My daddy brought me a new toy,
A Luton fan on a piece of string,
He told me to kick his f**king head in,
F**king head in,
F**king head in,
He told me to kick his f**king head in...

WHEN I WAS JUST A LITTLE BOY

(To the tune of Que Sera Sera)

When I was just a little boy,
I asked my mother what will I be,
Will I be Watford or Luton Town,
Here's what she said to me,
Wash your mouth out son,
And go get your fathers gun,
And shoot some Luton scum,
Shoot some Luton scum,
We hate Luton, we hate Luton...

WHERE WERE YOU

(To the tune of Bread of Heaven)

Where were you, where were you,
Where were you when Deeney scored,
Where were you when Deeney scored...

WHERE'S YOUR FAMOUS ATMOSPHERE

(To the tune of Bread of Heaven)

Where's your famous,
Where's your famous,
Where's your famous atmosphere,
Where's your famous atmosphere...

WHO ARE YA

Who are ya, who are ya, who are ya...

WHO LET THE HORNS OUT

(To the tune of Who Let The Dogs Out)

Who, who, who let the Horns out,
Who, who, who let the Horns out,
Who, who, who let the Horns out...

WHO THE HELL ARE YOU

(To the tune of Bread of Heaven)

Who the f**k,
Who the f**k,
Who the f**king hell are you,
Who the f**king hell are you...

WHO'S THAT STANDING ON THE CORNER

Who's that standing on the corner,
Luton sh*te scarf round your neck,
Watford fans are gonna get ya,
And we'll break your f**king neck.

WINGS OF A SPARROW

(To tune of My Bonnie Lies Over The Ocean)

If I had the wings of a sparrow,
If I had the ar*e of a crow,
I'd fly over Luton tomorrow,
And sh*t on the b**tards below, below,
Sh*t on, sh*t on,
I'd sh*t on the b**tards below, below,
Sh*t on, sh*t on, I'd sh*t on the b**tards below...

WON'T GET PAID

(To the tune of Tom Hark by Piranhas)

You won't get paid 'cos you play for Leeds,
You won't get paid 'cos you play for Leeds...

WOULDN'T IT BE LOVERLY

(To the tune of Wouldn't It Be Loverly)

All I want is a bottle and a brick,
A Watford scarf and a walking stick,
A Luton fan to punch and kick,
Ohhh wouldn't it be loverly...

YELLOW ARMY

Yellow Army, Yellow Army, Yellow Army...

YELLOW RED AND BLACK ARMY

Yellow Red And Black Army,
Yellow Red And Black Army...

YELLOWS

Yellows, Yellows, Yellows...

YOU ARE MY WATFORD

(To the tune of You Are My Sunshine)

You are my Watford, my only Watford,
You make me happy, when skies are grey,
I never noticed how much I love you,
Till you take my Watford away...

YOU KNOW YOU ARE

(To the tune of Go West)

You're sh*t and you know you are,
You're sh*t and you know you are,
You're sh*t and you know you are,
You're sh*t and you know you are...

YOU WHAT

You what, you what, you what...

YOU'RE NOT SINGING ANYMORE

(To the tune of Bread of Heaven)

You're not singing,
You're not singing,
You're not singing anymore,
You're not singing anymore...

YOUR GROUND'S BIG FOR YOU

(To the tune of La Donna È Mobile)

Your ground's too big for you,
Your ground's too big for you,
Your ground's too big for you,
Your ground's too big for you...

YOUR SUPPORT

(To the tune of Bread of Heaven)

Your support,
Your support,
Your support is f**king sh*t,
Your support is f**king sh*t...

YOU'RE GOING HOME

You're going home in a Watford ambulance,
You're going home in a Watford ambulance.

YOU'RE GONNA GET

You're gonna get your f**king head kicked in,
You're gonna get your f**king head kicked in...

YOU'RE NOT FAMOUS ANYMORE

(To the tune of Bread of Heaven)

You're not famous,
You're not famous,
You're not famous anymore,
You're not famous anymore...

YOU'RE NOT FIT TO REFEREE

(To the tune of Bread of Heaven)

You're not fit,
You're not fit,
You're not fit to referee,
You're not fit to referee...

YOU'RE NOT FIT TO WEAR

(To the tune of Bread of Heaven)

You're not fit to,
You're not fit to,
You're not fit to wear that shirt,
You're not fit to wear that shirt...

YOU'RE NOT VERY GOOD

(To the tune of Knees Up Mother Brown)

You're not very good,
You're not very good,
You're not very,
You're not very,
You're not very good...

YOU'RE SUPPOSED TO BE AT HOME

(To the tune of Bread of Heaven)

You're supposed to,
You're supposed to,
You're supposed to be at home,
You're supposed to be at home...

Printed in Great Britain
by Amazon